Floods

Michele Ingber Drohan

The Rosen Publishing Group's
PowerKids Press™
New York

Published in 1999 by The Rosen Publishing Group, Inc.
29 East 21st Street, New York, NY 10010

First Edition

Book Design: Danielle Primiceri

Photo Credits: Cover TK; p. 5 © J.R. Tesa/International Stock; p. 6 © Bradley/Leverett/FPG International; p. 9 © W. Faidley/International Stock; p. 10 © Laurance B. Aiuppy/FPG International; p. 13 © Buddy Mays/International Stock; p. 14 © Hank de Lespinasse/The Image Bank; p. 17 © Wayne Aldridge/International Stock; p. 18 © Reuters/The Brisbane Courier Mail/Archive; p. 21 © Guido Alberto Rossi/The Image Bank.

Drohan, Michele Ingber.
    Floods / Michele Ingber Drohan.
         p.   cm.— (Natural disasters)
    Includes index.
    Summary: Examines the nature, origins, and dangers of floods and discusses how to prevent them and protect against them.
    ISBN 0-8239-5288-6
    1. Floods—Juvenile literature. [1. Floods.] I. Title. II. Series.
GB1399.D76 1998
551.48'9—dc21
                                                 98-9267
                                                  CIP
                                                      AC

Manufactured in the United States of America

Contents

Water

Water is very important to people, plants, and animals. We all need water to live. Most of the water on Earth is found in the ocean. Ocean water is the **source** (SORSS) for most of the rain. But how does ocean water become rain?

When the sun heats the water in the ocean, the water **evaporates** (ee-VA-puh-rayts). This means that it changes into moisture. This moisture rises into the sky. As it travels up, the moisture cools and forms clouds. These clouds make the rain that falls back into the ocean. Then the **cycle** (SY-kul) starts all over again.

Three-quarters of planet Earth is covered with water. ▶

4

What Causes Floods?

A flood happens when water from a river, lake, or ocean overflows onto the land around it. Too much rain or melting snow are the main causes of floods. Sometimes the soil in the ground can make a flood worse. This is because when rain falls, the soil usually soaks it up like a sponge. But when the soil can't soak up any more water, it will send extra water into a river. This happens a lot during the winter because frozen soil can't soak up water. Floods often happen when the warm weather of spring melts snow before the ground has time to **thaw** (THAW).

◄ This house in Malibu, California, was destroyed in 1983 during a flood that happened after a storm.

Flash Flood!

It's hard to believe, but a flood can happen in just a few minutes. This is called a flash flood. Flash floods happen after heavy periods of rain caused by thunderstorms or **hurricanes** (HUR-ih-kaynz). They can also happen when a dam or a **levee** (LEH-vee) breaks. This causes a large amount of water to flood an area in a very short time. Flash floods are not common, but they are very **dangerous** (DAYN-jer-us). Flash floods don't give people much time to escape, and many people die in them each year. In 1889 a dam broke above Johnstown, Pennsylvania. Thousands of people died in the flash flood that followed. This was one of the worst flash floods in history.

Large thunderstorms can drop huge amounts of water in one place in a short time. Because of this, thunderstorms are a common cause of flash floods. ▶

Natural Flood Control

Floods are a natural part of any river. All rivers flood at some time. This is why rivers have flood plains. Flood plains are natural flat lands on each side of the river. They are nature's way of controlling floods. Flood plains hold the water that flows over the river's banks. When the river's water level falls, the water in the flood plains slowly flows back into the river. Flooding actually helps the river by getting rid of **sediment** (SEH-duh-ment) that has gathered in it. Flooding cleans the river of extra sand, mud, and rocks. However, flooding becomes dangerous when people build their towns and homes in flood plains.

◀ *These flat lands are the flood plains of this river.*

The Mighty Mississippi

The Mississippi River is one of the longest rivers in the world. It runs for 2,350 miles, through ten states. Throughout history Americans have **depended** (duh-PEN-ded) on the Mississippi River for jobs in trade, shipping, and **agriculture** (A-grih-kul-cher). But even though people have tried to **tame** (TAYM) the river, it is too powerful to control.

From April to July of 1927 the river flooded again and again. Millions of acres of land were underwater. In some places, the water rose to 30 feet above ground. Close to 1 million people lost their homes. It was the worst flood in United States history.

The first steamboat, such as this one, traveled down the Mississippi River in 1811. Since then, the Mississippi has been a very ▶ important waterway in the United States.

Building Levees

Levees are **barriers** (BAR-ee-erz) built along the sides of a river to stop it from flooding. Levees are made of earth and sandbags. They raise the banks of the river so it can hold more water. The Mississippi River has a long history of flooding. As a result, many levees have been built to protect the people who live in the river's flood plains. But some **experts** (EK-sperts) think that levees increase the level of danger. Levees let a river hold more water than it naturally could. So if a levee breaks, the flooding is much worse than if the levee had never been built at all.

◀ *In addition to levees, flood control channels, such as these in Nevada, are often built to help avoid flooding.*

Flood Watches and Warnings

It usually takes many hours or days for a flood to happen. If it has been raining for a long time, an area may have a flood watch. This means that there is the possibility of a flood. But if a flood is already happening or is about to happen, there will be a flood warning. Television and radio stations will alert people to what they should do. Sometimes people only need to move themselves and their belongings to higher places in their homes. But if the flood is very serious, often people must **evacuate** (ee-VA-kyoo-wayt) as soon as possible.

These homes on the Willamette River in Portland, Oregon, had to be evacuated during this flood. The families who left lost many of their belongings in the flood. ▶

Rescue

Sometimes people get trapped during a flood. If the water rises very high, people may even be trapped on the roofs of their houses. This may happen during a flash flood when there is no warning. Rescue teams must be sent out to save people. Helicopters are used to find people in danger. Then firefighters use small boats to rescue them and take them to safety. Local churches and schools are often turned into shelters. There, rescuers and other **volunteers** (vah-lun-TEERZ) will give people food, clothes, and a place to stay until the water level goes down. That may take days, weeks, or even months. After the water has gone down people return to their homes to see what **damage** (DA-mij) has been done.

◀ *These people were allowed to take only one suitcase with them when they were rescued.*

Deltas

Many people think that floods only cause harm. But sometimes floods help people by forming **deltas** (DEL-tuz). A delta is an area of land that is formed from the sediment at the bottom of a river. During a flood, most of the sediment flows onto the flood plains. But the rest of it runs to the end of the river and into the ocean. Over time the sediment builds up and creates new land at the end of the river. That land is called a delta. Because of the sediment, deltas are very **fertile** (FER-tul), and provide good farmland. The city of New Orleans in Louisiana is on the delta formed by the Mississippi River.

This is the city of Alexandria, Egypt. It is built on the delta formed by the Nile River, which is the longest river in the world. ▶

Staying Safe in a Flood

Many people live in areas that flood again and again. These people must always be ready for an **emergency** (ee-MER-jen-see). The American Red Cross helps people by giving them tips on how to stay safe in emergencies. They tell people how to make a flood safety kit. This kit should include canned food, bottled water, flashlights with batteries, a battery-powered radio, and a first-aid kit. Families should also have a place to go if they have to leave their homes. Remember, it's not safe to walk, swim, or drive in flood waters. Even though floods can be dangerous and scary, they are an important part of nature.

Web Sites:

You can learn more about floods at this Web site: http://www.fema.gov/kids/

Glossary

agriculture (A-grih-kul-cher) Farming.

barrier (BAR-ee-er) Something, such as a levee, that stands in the way of something else, such as flood waters.

cycle (SY-kul) The period of time in which an event happens again and again.

damage (DA-mij) To harm or hurt something or someone.

dangerous (DAYN-jer-us) Something that can cause harm.

delta (DEL-tuh) The place at the end of a river where sediment is left.

depend (duh-PEND) To rely on someone or something.

emergency (ee-MER-jen-see) An event that happens with little or no warning, where help is needed very fast.

evacuate (ee-VA-kyoo-wayt) To leave an area that is dangerous.

evaporate (ee-VA-puh-rayt) To change from a liquid to a gas.

expert (EK-spert) A person with a lot of knowledge about a certain subject.

fertile (FER-tul) Good for growing produce, such as fruits and vegetables.

hurricane (HUR-ih-kayn) A storm with strong winds and heavy rain.

levee (LEH-vee) A raised bank to stop a river from overflowing.

sediment (SEH-duh-ment) Material that settles at the bottom of a liquid.

source (SORSS) Where something starts.

tame (TAYM) To make a wild person, animal, or thing gentle.

thaw (THAW) To change from being frozen to liquid, such as when ice and snow melt.

volunteer (vah-lun-TEER) Someone who chooses to do something, such as help others, for no pay.

Index